Listening comprehension for Intermediate learners books

By:

Kamolova Shaxlo

Nutfillayev Bekzod

© Taemeer Publications LLC
Listening comprehension for intermediate learners books
by: Kamolova Shaxlo / Nutfillayev Bekzod
Edition: August '2023
Publisher:
Taemeer Publications LLC (Michigan, USA / Hyderabad, India)

ISBN 978-93-5872-144-7

© Taemeer Publications

Book : *Listening comprehension for intermediate learners books*

Author/s : Kamolova Shaxlo
Nutfillayev Bekzod

Publisher : Taemeer Publications

Year : '2023

Pages : 36

Title Design : *Taemeer Web Design*

Table of Content

- Introduction
- English is the global language
- Uzbekistan is my motherland
- National costumes
- Clothes
- Magazines and newspapers
- Letters
- Restaurants and cafes
- The USA
- Hobbies and activities
- Cinema
- Popular music
- Communications
- Literature

INTRODUCTION

"Knowing the language, youwill acknowledge the world", says our wise nation. Naturally, everyone who possesses foreign languages has a number of opportunities such as getting training in foreign countries or simply traveling through them, getting acquainted with the culture, history, traditions and customs of different peoples and thereby broadening their horizons and increasing enthusiasm to learn deeply modern knowledge and professions. Today, with pride, we can say that the interest of young people in Uzbekistan to study foreign languages has increased, than ever. Many of them have the ability to speak 4-5 languages. Decree of the first President of Uzbekistan I.A. Karimov "On measures of further improvement of the –system of studying-foreign languages-of-December-10.2012- serves as the main model in this work. It should be noted that this document includes all the parameters of teaching foreign languages, especially English.

From 2013-2014 academic year, a phased study of foreign languages -mostly English -from the first class in the form of games oforal lessons began, in the second class-with the development of the alphabet,reading andgrammar. Receiving a monthly supplement to the official salary of teachers of a foreign language, as well as exemption with the award of a maximum score of graduates of secondary educational institutions with a level of A2 and higher- upon admission to secondary special, professional educational institutions,- applicants with a level of Bl and higher- upon admission to the fhigher education educational institutions, applicants with a level of Cl and above - upon admission to the magistracy of higher educational institutions, general educators, secondary special professors, (Decree of the Cabinet of Ministers of 11.08. 2017 No. 610 On measures to further improve the quality of teaching foreign languages in educational institutions) is considered a true improvement and continuation of the above Decree. It is known that students of primary classes initially learn the skills of speaking, and then begin to work on grammar.

On this basis, teachers of foreign languages should have the skills to use new pedagogical technologies and teaching methods. To fulfill this goal, each of us must continuously work on ourselves. In addition, the work of students with topics on various topical issues will serve as a support for the profound mastering of the skills of speaking foreign languages.

English is the global language

A headline of this kind must have appeared in a thousand newspapers and magazines in recent years. 'English Rules' is an actual example, presenting to the world an uncomplicated scenario suggesting the universality of the language's spread and the likelihood of its continuation. A statement prominently displayed in the body of the associated article, memorable chiefly for its alliterative ingenuity, reinforces the initial impression: 'The British Empire may be in full retreat with the handover of Hong Kong. But from Bengal to Belize and Las Vegas to Lahore, the language of the sceptred isle is rapidly becoming the first global lingua franca.' Millennial retrospectives and prognostications continued in the same vein, with several major newspapers and magazines finding in the subject of the English language an apt symbol for the themes of globalization, diversification, progress and identity addressed in their special editions. Television programmes and series, too, addressed the issue, and achieved world-wide audiences.

Certainly, by the turn of the century, the topic must have made contact with millions of popular intuitions at a level which had simply not existed a decade before. These are the kinds of statement which seem so obvious that most people would give them hardly a second thought. Of course English is a global language, they would say. You hear it on television spoken by politicians from all over the world. Wherever you travel, you see English signs and advertisements. Whenever you enter a hotel or restaurant in a foreign city, they will understand English, and there will be an English menu. Indeed, if there is anything to wonder about at all, they might add, it is why such headlines should still be newsworthy. But English is news. The language continues to make news daily in many countries. And the headline isn't stating the obvious. For what does it mean, exactly? Is it saying that everyone in the world speaks English?

This is certainly not true, as we shall see. Is it saying, then, that every country in the world recognizes English as an official language? This is not true either. So what does it mean to say that a language is a global language? Why is English the language which is usually cited in this connection? How did the situation arise? And could it change? Or is it the case that, once a language becomes a global language, it is there for ever? These are fascinating questions to explore, whether your first language is English or not. If English is your mother tongue, you may have mixed feelings about the way English is spreading around the world. You may feel pride, that your language is the one which has been so successful; but your pride may be tinged with concern, when you realize that people in other countries may not want to use the language in the same way that you do, and are changing it to suit themselves. We are all sensitive to the way other people use (it is often said, abuse) 'our' language.

Deeply held feelings of ownership begin to be questioned. Indeed, if there is one predictable consequence of a language becoming a global language, it is that nobody owns it any more. Or rather, everyone who has learned it now owns it – 'has a share in it' might be more accurate – and has the right to use it in the way they want. This fact alone makes many people feel uncomfortable, even vaguely resentful. 'Look what the Americans have done to English' is a not uncommon comment found in the letter-columns of the British press. But similar comments can be heard in the USA when people encounter the sometimes striking variations in English which are emerging all over the world. And if English is not your mother tongue, you may still have mixed feelings about it. You may be strongly motivated to learn it, because you know it will put you in touch with more people than any other language; but at the same time you know it will take a great deal of effort to master it, and you may begrudge that effort.

Having made progress, you will feel pride in your achievement, and savour the communicative power you have at your disposal, but may none the less feel that mother-tongue speakers of English have an unfair advantage over you. And if you live in a country where the survival of your own language is threatened by the success of English, you may feel envious, resentful, or angry. You may strongly object to the naivety of the populist account, with its simplistic and often suggestively triumphalist tone.

Uzbekistan is my motherland

My country is Uzbekistan. It is a multinational country. The population of Uzbekistan is more than 33 million people. There are a lot of nations: Uzbeks, Russians, Tatars, Korean and etc. All people are friendly and respect each other. When people meet they kiss each other and shake hands. The Republic has its own flag, hymn, emblem and Constitution. Uzbekistan has rich history. Great scientists, commanders, medics and writers belonged to our Holy Land. The state language is Uzbek, but people also speak in Russian, Tajik and other languages. Alisher Navoi is the founder of the Uzbek literature –language. He was a great medic and scientist. He is known all over the world. Amir Temur was a great commander and ruler. He played an important role for our country. There are a lot of ancient cities in Uzbekistan. Bukhara, Khiva, Samarkand, Shakhrisabs and others. Many tourists like visiting Uzbekistan. Our country is rich in fruit and vegetables. Uzbekistan is one of the most important producers of cotton and silk. The climate of our country is continental. Summer is a hot and dry season. Winter is not usually cold. Spring and Autumn are the most pleasant and warm seasons. Uzbekistan has a great economy. The country is developing in various spheres. Education system is the most important branch. Schools, colleges and universities are full of students. There are a lot of parks, museums, theatres in our country. I am proud of my country, because Uzbekistan is a friendly, peaceful and hospitable country.

National costumes

Each country has its own traditions and national costumes. Uzbek national clothes are very bright, beautiful and cozy. Uzbek clothes are a part of rich cultural traditions and life style of Uzbek people. The basis of national men's suit is achapan, the quilted robe, tied with a kerchief. Traditional men's cap is tubeteika or duppi in Uzbek. Traditional Uzbek women's suit consists of plain khan-atlas tunic-dress and wide trousers.

Usually Uzbek people dress national costumes on special days or holidays. For example, on Navruz or Kurban Khait holidays. In Russia, traditional costumes always have been an important component of national culture and traditions. The Russian women's costume is "rubakha" or "sarafan". It is the element of Russian folk culture. One of the most common type of festive head-dress was the "kokoshnik". Men's costume consists of a long shirt, trousers, ъ belt, and bast shoes. National clothes of English people differ from Uzbek ones. For example, traditional dress for men in Scotland is a kilt with shirt, waistcoat and tweedjacket, stockings with garter flashes, brogue shoes. For the ladies the typical Welsh costume consists of a hat, made of black felt, with a high crown and wide brim. All national costumes are wonderful and show us the culture of country.

Clothes

"Clothes are an important part of modern life. It's hard to imagine how people can live without clothes. There are different styles of clothes nowadays and people can choose what to wear on different occasions. I think it is very important for everyone to find their own style. As for me, I have a good collection of clothes in my wardrobe. There is a couple of school suits of classic style. Then I have some jeans and T-shirts for every day. And at last, I have a couple of bright dresses for parties or special occasions.

Most of all I like wearing jeans with T-shirts. I think that clothes tell a lot about people and can make a strong impression. So if they are tidy and nice the impression will be positive. There are four seasons in a year. Each of them brings different weather and requires different dresses. The choice of clothes also depends on weather conditions. In winter, for example, it's important to have a warm coat and a pair of boots. A jacket and rubber boots would be nice for. spring and autumn. However, my favorite time is summer, when everyone.

Attitude to clothing at different times has changed. Luxurious outfits were worn by richer population, and the poor wore scant, unattractive, cheap clothes. Many rich people tend to show their superiority. By clothes, you can determine where a person works, whathe~likes to io~and call character traits..

Clothing can be divided by season, by appointment, by quality. For. physical work, people prefer simple, dark, comfortable, easy-to-wash clothes. On parties, graduation, banquet, birthdays people are usually dressed elegantly. It is important that the clothes on the man were dressed for the season, and also clean and neat in appearance. There are different types of clothing: business, sports, medical, professional and home look.

Our clothesreflect on our social status. For example ifyou are a business lady you should be dressed appropriately, it is preferable to wear well branded clothes. Some people spend a lot oftime on buying clothes It means shopping for clothes can be a goodTherapy in case oftroubles, but you shouldn't become a.shopaholic and buy everything you see, the sense ofstyle of clothes is extremely important.It is important to keep to your style of dress.

Magazines and newspapers

Newspaper and magazines play a very important role in our life. Magazine is a collection of articles and stories. – Usually magazines, also contain illustrations. Magazines provide information on a wide range of topics such as business, culture, hobbies, medicine, religion, science, and sports. Some magazines entertain their readers with fiction, poetry, photography or articles about TV or movie stars. Children's magazines contain stories, jokes, articles on subjects especially interesting for children and instructions for making games or useful items. Hobby magazines are intended for collectors of coins, stamps, and other items; people interested in certain sports or games. Intellectual magazines provide analysis of current cultural and political events. Women's magazines have articles about child-raising, fashion trends, romance. They show ideas on cooking and home decorating. Newspaper is a publication that presents and comments on the news. Newspapers play an important role in shaping public .opinion and informing people of current events. My family and I are fond of reading newspapers. At our flat you can always find different magazines and newspapers lying everywhere. There are political, economical, informational, reading for mind and other newspapers and magazines about all spheres of life. We don't like to eject old magazines because there is always interesting and useful information that one-day can be used.

Letters

A letter is one person's written message to another concerning some matter of common matter. In the 19th century, the letter was one of the main means of communication. It was in the letter that you could describe feelings and thoughts. There are different types of letters such as formal letters and informal ones. Factually, the process ofsending letters began from ancient times. Letters have existed from the time of ancient India, ancient Egypt, through Rome, Greece and China. At that time they were written on a various materials, including metal, lead, wax-coated wooden tablets, animal skin and papyrus. Initially, the letter was called a handwritten text message on paper or other medium (clay shard, sheet of parchment or piece ofbirch bark). Currently, the letter also means the message that is generated and or transmitted electronically (e.g. via email) or SMS (mobile phone). Such a letter can also contain not only text, but also various multimedia elements (for example, images, video and audio recordings). As communication technology has diversified, posted letters have become less important. Today, the internet, by means of email, plays a large part in written communications. However, a piece of writing in which the warmth, friendship, love or solidarity of the writer can be felt, never could be replaced by printed letters.

Restaurants and cafes

Today restaurants and cafes are popular industry in the world. Different types of restaurants offer delicious food and comfortable atmosphere for people. In restaurants people can also meet and communicate with their friends, relatives or business partners. There are many types of restaurants. They are divided into groups for a price class, for a service type (fast food, a la carte), for a type of the country (Italian, Chinese, Japanese, Indian and others). There are many traditional restaurants. The service is usually excellent and friendly, waiters help you to relax. For example, in the Italian restaurant you find many kinds of pasta, vegetables, cheese. Uzbek restaurants can offer many kinds of wonderful national meals. Cafes are also popular nowadays. It is a place where people can eat delicious and inexpensive food. In the cafe we can have breakfast and lunch, we can go there with family or meet up with friends. Modern cafes and restaurants provide different types of entertainment. Some of them have arena for children with different toys. In restaurants people can enjoy a show or music. You can taste all types of food in restaurants - you can taste homemade cakes, fish, beefsteaks, pasta and others. I think that restaurants are an important part of public life.

The USA

The United States of America was founded in 1776. This country is situated in the central part of North American continent. It's the fourth largest country in the world (afterRussia, Canada andChina). Itstretches from the Pacific to the Atlantic Ocean. It also includes Alaska in the north and Hawaii in the Pacific Ocean. The total area of the country is about nine and a halfmillion square kilometers. The USA borders on Canadain the north and on Mexico in the south. It also has a sea-border with Russia. The climate of the country varies greatly. The coldest regions are in the north. The climate of Alaska is arctic. The climate ofthe central part is continental. The south has a subtropical climate. Hot winds blowing from the Gulf of Mexico often bring typhoons.

The climate along the Pacific coast is much warmer than that ofthe Atlantic coast. America's largestrivers are the Mississippi, the Missouri, the Rio Grande and the Columbia. The Great Lakes on the border with Canada are the largest and deepest in the USA. The population of the country is more than 326 million. The USA is called the "nation ofimmigrants". There are many big cities in the USA, such as New York, Chicago, Los Angeles, Philadelphia, Dallas, Boston, etc. The capital of the USA is Washington in the District of Columbia (D.C.). It is an administrative city without much industry. Washington has many famous monuments in the streets and squares. One of them is Abraham Lincoln memorial. In the very centre ofthe city there is The Capitol, where the Congress meets. It is very high and beautiful building with white marble columns. Not far from the Capitol there is the Library ofCongress. The Library holds about 5 million books. In Washington, DC, 1600 Pennsylvania Avenue is a very special address. It's the address of the White House, the home ofthe President ofthe United States. Originally the White House was grey and was called the Presidential Palace. It was built from 1792 to 1800. At this time, the city of Washington itself was being built. It was to be the nation's new capital city. George Washington, the first president, and Pierre Charles L'Enfant, a French engineer, chose the place for the new city. L'Enfant then planned the city and the President's home was an important part ofthe plan. The USA is a highly developed industrial country. It's the world's leading producer of copper and oil and the world's second producer ofiron ore and coal. Among the most important manufacturing industries are aircraft, cars, textiles, radio and television sets, armaments, furniture and paper. The United States is a federal union of 50 states, each of which has its own government. The seat- of the central (federal) government is Washington, DC. According to the US Constitution the powers ofthe govern-ment are divided into 3 branches: the executive, headed by the President, the legislative, exercised by the Congress, and the judicial. The Congress consists of the Senate and the House of Representatives. There are two main political parties in the USA: the Republican and the Democratic, though there's hardly any difference between their political lines.

Hobbies and activities

Hobby is what a person loves to do in his free time. Each person has his or her own hobby. Every person chooses a hobby according to character and taste and life becomes more interesting. Different people like different things, they have different hobbies either. Sport is a very important part ofour life. Many people go in for sports; they do jogging, walking, swimming, skating, skiing, train themselves in clubs and different sections. Physical training is an important subject at school. Pupils play volleyball, football, basketball. I also go in for sports and I like playing tennis. I play it every day. I have been going in that type of sport for 5 years. Tennis became very popular now. I take part in different competitions. To be in a good shape I do jogging every morning and do my morning exercises. I do not understand people who say that they like sport, but they only watch it on TV. People who go in for sports, feel much better, look much better, and sleep much better.. Their physical appearance is also different from others. They will be slimmer and trimmer. And what is even more important is that they will not get sick often. Why do I go in for sports? Because I think it is very important for a man to be strong and well-built. Sport is not for the weak, because, you have to learn how to lose, and it's not easy. My favourite proverb says: "A sound mind in a sound body".

Hobby is a favorite occupation of a person in his or her free time. People are different so they have hobbies of various kinds. Somebody likes to knit or sew things, others like to make everything with their hands or to draw, to take pictures and so on. Many children and grown-ups are fond of collecting something. They collect old coins, postcards, toys, stamps and so on. This type of occupation is called hobby. Hobby helps people to relax, to forget about their troubles and to have a goodTiine. My hobby is learning English. Nowadays it's especially important to know foreign languages because we need it for our work, for travelling abroad. Everyone who knows foreign languages can speak to people from other countries, read foreign authors' masterpieces in original that makes our outlook wider. Now English has become the world's most important' language in politics, science, trade and cultural relations. English is the language of computers. Learning English for pleasure includes listening to my favorite English songs (mostly I prefer Enrique Iglesias's songs), chatting with my pen-friends from England, New Zealand, Canada and other countries in the Internet. All these things make my life exciting. I think my hobby is very useful and interesting.

Cinema

The new technologies which followed the discovery of electrical power fundamentally altered the nature of home and public entertainment, and provided fresh directions for the development of the English language. Broadcasting was obviously one of these, but that medium was never – according to the influential views of Lord Reith – to be identified solely with the provision of entertainment. This observation did not apply in the case of the motion picture industry. The technology of this industry has many roots in Europe and America during the nineteenth century, with Britain and France providing an initial impetus to the artistic and commercial development of the cinema from 1895. However, the years preceding and during the First World War stunted the growth of a European film industry, and dominance soon passed to America, which oversaw from 1915 the emergence of the feature film, the star system, the movie mogul, and the grand studio, all based in Hollywood, California. As a result, when sound was added to the technology in the late 1920s, it was the English language which suddenly came to dominate the movie world. It is difficult to find accurate data, but several publications of the period provide clues. For example, in 1933 appeared the first edition of The picturegoer's who's who and encyclopaedia of the screen today. Of the 44 studios listed, 32 were American or British (the others were

German and French). Of the 2,466 artistes listed, only 85(3 per cent) were making movies in languages other than English.

Of the 340 directors, 318 (94 per cent) were involved only in English-language works. As an English-language reference book, there is bound to be some bias in the coverage – few movie stars are listed from nonEuropean countries, for example – but the overall impression is probably not far from the truth. Despite the growth of the film industry in other countries in later decades, English-language movies still dominate the medium, with Hollywood coming to rely increasingly on a small number of annual productions aimed at huge audiences – such as Star Wars, Titanic and The Lord of the Rings. It is unusual to find a blockbuster movie produced in a language other than English. In 2002, according to the listings in the BFI film and television handbook, over 80 per cent of all feature films given a theatrical release were in English. The Oscar system has always been Englishlanguage oriented (though the category of best foreign film was recognized in 1947), but there is a strong English-language presence in most other film festivals too. Half of the Best Film awards ever given at the Cannes Film Festival, for example, have been to English-language productions.

By the mid-1990s, according to film critic David Robinson in an Encyclopaedia Britannica review, the USA controlled about 85per cent of the world film market, with Hollywood films dominating the box offices in most countries. A cinema in Denmark would very likely be showing the same range of films as one in Spain, and most would be English-language films (usually subtitled). A notable development was to see this dominance manifest itself even in countries where there has been a strong national tradition of film-making, such as Japan, France, Italy and Germany. Before 1990, France was continuing to attract majority audiences for its own films (the only European country to do so); in recent years, French-language films may account for as little as 30 per cent of the national box office. The influence of movies on the viewing audience is uncertain, but many observers agree with the view of the German director Wim Wenders: 'People increasingly believe in what they see and they buy what they believe in... People use, drive, wear, eat and buy what they see in the movies.' If this is so, then the fact that most movies are made in the English language must surely be significant, at least in the long term.

Popular music

The cinema was one of two new entertainment technologies which emerged at the end of the nineteenth century: the other was the recording industry. Here too the English language was early in evidence. When in 1877 Thomas A. Edison devised the phonograph, the first machine that could both record and reproduce sound, the first words to be recorded were 'What God hath wrought', followed by the words of the nursery-rhyme 'Mary had a little lamb'. Most of the subsequent technical developments took place in the USA. Gramophone records soon came to replace cylinders. The first US patent for magnetic tape was as early as 1927. Columbia Records introduced the long-playing (LP) disk in 1948. All the major recording companies in popular music had Englishlanguage origins.

The oldest active record label is the US firm Columbia (from 1898); others are HMV (originally British), merged in 1931 with Columbia to form EMI. Other labels include Brunswick, established in the USA in 1916, and Decca, established in Britain in 1929. Radio sets around the world hourly testify to the dominance of English in the popular music scene today. Many people make their first contact with English in this way. It is a dominance which is a specifically twentieth-century phenomenon, but the role of English in this genre starts much earlier. During the nineteenth century, popular music was embedded within the dance halls, beer halls, and popular theatres of innumerable European cities, producing thousands of songs whose content ranged from the wildly comic and satirical to the desperately sentimental.

The British music hall was a major influence on popular trends – much more so, it is thought, than the French and German cabarets and operettas of the period. Travelling British entertainers visited the USA, which developed its own music hall traditions in the form of vaudeville. Touring minstrel groups became popular from the middle of the nineteenth century. Songwriters such as Stephen Foster found their compositions (over 200 hits, including 'Old Folks at Home', 'Camptown Races', and 'Beautiful Dreamer') circulating on an unprecedented scale through the rapidly growing network of theatres. By the turn of the century, Tin Pan Alley (the popular name for the Broadway-centred song-publishing industry) was a reality, and was soon known worldwide as the chief source of US popular music. A similar trend can be seen in relation to the more 'upmarket' genres. During the early twentieth century, European light opera (typified by Strauss and Offenbach) developed an English-language dimension. Several major composers were immigrants to the USA, such as the Czech-born Rudolf Friml (who arrived in 1906) and Hungarian-born Sigmund Romberg (who arrived in 1909), or they were the children of immigrants (such as George Gershwin). The 1920s proved to be a remarkable decade for the operetta, as a result, with such famous examples as Romberg's The Student Prince (1924) and Friml's Rose Marie.

The same decade also saw the rapid growth of the musical, a distinctively US product, and the rise to fame of such composers as Jerome Kern and George Gershwin, and later Cole Porter and Richard Rodgers. The rapidly growing broadcasting companies were greedy for fresh material, and thousands of new works each year found an international audience in ways that could not have been conceived of a decade before. The availability of mass-produced gramophone records allowed the works of these composers ('songs from the shows') to travel the world in physical form. Soon the words of the hit songs were being learned by heart and reproduced with varying accents in cabarets and music halls all over Europe – as well as in the homes of the well-to-do. Jazz, too, influenced so much by the folk blues of black plantation workers, had its linguistic dimension. Blues singers such as Ma Rainey and Bessie Smith were part of the US music-hall scene from the early years of the twentieth century. Other genres emerged – hillbilly songs, country music, gospel songs, and a wide range of folk singing. The vocal element in the dance music of such swing bands as Glenn Miller's swept the world in the 1930s and 1940s. And, in due course, the words and beat of rhythm and blues grew into rock and roll. When modern popular music arrived, it was almost entirely an English scene. The pop groups of two chief English-speaking nations were soon to dominate the recording world: Bill Haley and the Comets and Elvis Presley in the USA; the Beatles and the Rolling Stones in the UK. Mass audiences for pop singers became a routine feature of the world scene from the 1960s. No other single source has spread the English language around the youth of the world so rapidly and so pervasively. In 1996, Nick Reynolds, a popular music producer of the BBC World Service, commented: 'Pop music is virtually the only field in which the British have led the world in the past three decades', and adds, echoing the accolade made some 200 years ago (p. 80), 'Britain is still the pop workshop of the planet'.

In the 2000s, the English-language character of the international pop music world is extraordinary. Although every country has its popular singers, singing in their own language, only a few manage to break through into the international arena, and in order to do so it seems they need to be singing in English. The 1990 edition of The Penguin encyclopedia of popular music was an instructive guide to the 1990s decade: of the 557 pop groups it included, 549 (99 per cent) worked entirely or predominantly in English; of the 1,219 solo vocalists, 1,156 (95 per cent) sang in English. The mother tongue of the singers was apparently irrelevant. The entire international career of ABBA, the Swedish group with over twenty hit records in the 1970s, was in English. Most contributions to the annual Eurovision Song Contest are in English –17 titles out of 24 in 2002.

These days, the sound of the English language, through the medium of popular song, is heard wherever there is a radio set. It is a commonplace tourist experience to hear a familiar English refrain in a coffee bar, bus station or elevator, or simply issuing from the window of a house on almost any street in any town. Often, it is a source of despair. We travel to 'get away from it all', and 'it' follows us everywhere we go. We enter a local nightclub in our holiday destination, and all we hear is the current top twenty. 'Happy birthday to you' is widely sung at children's birthday parties in many countries. Finding genuinely local music can be extremely difficult. Several commentators have remarked on the way in which western popular music has threatened the life of ethnic musical traditions everywhere. At the same time, other commentators have drawn attention to the way popular music in the English language has had a profound and positive impact on the nature of modern popular culture in general.

As the lyrics (as distinct from the tunes) of Bob Dylan, Bob Marley, John Lennon, Joan Baez and others spread around the world, during the 1960s and 1970s, English for the younger generation in many countries became a symbol of freedom, rebellion and modernism. The social, political, and spiritual messages carried by the words (such as 'We Shall Overcome') resounded at gatherings in many countries, providing many people with a first – and often highly charged – experience of the unifying power of English in action. And the language has continued to play this role, being the medium of such international projects as 'Live Aid'.

Communications

If a language is a truly international medium, it is going to be most apparent in those services which deal directly with the task of communication – the postal and telephone systems and the electronic networks. Information about the use of English in these domains is not easy to come by, however. No one monitors the language in which we write our letters; there is no one noting the language we use when we talk on the phone. Only on the Internet, where messages and data can be left for indefinite periods of time, is it possible to develop an idea of how much of the world's everyday communications (at least, between computer-owners) is actually in English. There are various indirect methods of calculation, of course. We can draw up a list of those countries where English has special status (see chapter 2), and look at the pieces of mail sent, or the number of telephone calls made. Data of this kind are available, though hedged in with many qualifications. For example, using the information compiled in the 2002 Britannica Yearbook, it transpires that about 63 per cent of the world's mail in 2001 was being handled by English-status countries. However, information is not available for thirty-two countries, and those countries which have provided totals arrived at them in a variety of ways. One fact is plain: the amount of mail sent through just the US postal system that year (some 197 thousand million pieces) was larger than the total for all the non-English-speaking countries put together. Indeed, if the USA is matched against all other countries, it accounts for nearly half of the world's volume of postal traffic. Even if we assume that the proportion of the US population which speaks other languages (about 15per cent) never writes in English, we must still conclude that 40 per cent of the world's mail is in English, from the USA alone. A widely quoted statistic is that three-quarters of the world's mail is in English. It is certainly possible to arrive at this figure if we make guesses about the number of people in different countries who are involved in organizations which use English as an officia language, or which rely on English for correspondence. When scientists from any country write to each other, for example, the language they use is almost always going to be English. The figures for international mail are likely to reflect those for international associations cited above, where again English is widespread. But there are no precise calculations. Another widely quoted statistic is that about 80 per cent of the world's electronically stored information is currently in English. Figures of this kind relate to two kinds of data: information stored privately by individual firms and organizations, such as commercial businesses, libraries and security forces; and information made available through the Internet, whether for sending and receiving electronic mail, participating in discussion groups, or providing and accessing databases and data pages. Statistics of this kind have to be cautiously interpreted. They seem to be little more than extrapolations from computer sales and distribution patterns – and thus simply reflect the pioneering role of the USA in developing and marketing computational hardware and software. In particular, given the American origins of the Internet (as ARPANET, the Advanced Research Projects Agency network devised in the late 1960s), it is not surprising that most Internet hosts – 64 per cent, according to a Business Week survey – are to be found in the USA. A further 12.7 per cent were thought to be in other English-speaking countries. But there is no easy way of predicting the language of Internet users or documents from the location of their hosts. It is important for the theme of this book to see how English came to have such a dominant position on the Internet. ARPANET was conceived as a decentralized national network, its aim being to link important American academic and government institutions in a way which would survive local damage in the event of a major war. Its language was, accordingly, English; and when people in other countries began to form links with this network, it proved essential for them to use English. The dominance of this language was then reinforced when the service was opened up in the 1980s to private and commercial organizations, most of which were (for the reasons given earlier in this chapter) already communicating chiefly in English. There was also a technical reason underpinning the position of the language at this time. The first protocols devised to carry data on the Net were developed for the English alphabet, using a character set (called Latin 1) which had no diacritical marks and which was transmitted in a 7-bit ASCII code. An 8-bit code and a character set including diacritics (Latin 2) later became available, and more sophisticated protocols were devised with multilingualism in mind, but major problems have hindered their international implementation in a standardized way. Unicode, using a 16-bit code, allowed the representation of nearly 50,000 characters (version 3, rising to over 94,000 in version 3.1), but even this is not enough to handle the characters in all the world's languages, which have been estimated at over 170,000.33 There are problems of data representation and manipulation (especially involving the selection, encoding, and conversion of character sets), data display (handling such issues as the direction of a writing system, or the mapping of character codes into an appropriate range of images on screen), and data input (such as the use of different keyboard layouts and techniques). Several ad hoc solutions have been devised, but ad hoc solutions bring with them problems of compatibility, and this limits the ability of the World Wide Web to be truly interoperable – that is, enabling all servers and clients to communicate intelligently with each other, whatever the data source. Most browsers are still unable to handle multilingual data presentation. More than just diacritics is involved, as is evident from a consideration of such writing systems as Arabic, Chinese, Korean, Thai and Hindi, some of which require very large character sets. More than alphabetic text is involved: there are difficulties in handling conventions to do with money, dates, measurements, and other types of special setting which need to be anticipated. At present a truly multilingual World Wide Web remains a long-term goal – a Web where end users can expect to input data using their language of choice in a routine way, and can expect any server to receive and display the data without problems.34 In the meantime, English continues to be the chief lingua franca of the Internet – a position which during the 1990s began to be acknowledged in the popular media. For example, in April 1996 The New York Times carried an article by Michael Specter headed 'World, Wide, Web: English Words', in which the role of English was highlighted:

To study molecular genetics, all you need to get into the Harvard University Library, or the medical library at Sweden's Karolinska Institute, is a phone line and a computer. And, it turns out, a solid command of the English language. Because whether you are a French intellectual pursuing the cutting edge of international film theory, a Japanese paleobotanist curious about a newly discovered set of primordial fossils, or an American teen-ager concerned about Magic Johnson's jump shot, the Internet and World Wide Web really only work as great unifiers if you speak English.

Literature

1. Oxford Phrasal-Verbs Dictionary, Oxford University — press, 2001.
2. Английские фразовые глаголы: учебный справочник, Т.В. Митрошкина - Минск, Тетра Системе, 2011.
3. Oxford English, Russian-English Dictionary.
4. 400 тем по английскому языку для школьников, абитуриентов, студентов и преподавателей Куриленко Ю.В

Electronic resources:
1. abbreviations.yourdictionary.com.
2. Cambridge Dictionaries Online: http.//dictionaries.cambridge.org
3. English Lessons Phrasal Verbs: http.//carolinebrownenglishlessons.com
4. engmaster.ru
5. en.wikipedia.org
6. www.learnenglishbest.com
7. Lingvo: www.lingvo.ru
8. Longman English Dictionary Online: www.ldoceonline.com
9. Oxford Dictionary: www.taskoxford.com
10. www.alleng.org/english/engl.
11. www.spokenenglishpractice.com
12. www.cosmopolitan.com
13. www.native-english.ru
14. www.uza.uz

www.ingramcontent.com/pod-product-compliance
Lightning Source LLC
LaVergne TN
LVHW010418070526
838199LV00064B/5343